The Other Side of the Counter

THE OTHER SIDE OF THE COUNTER

36 Years of Serving Dodger Dogs
and Getting Grilled!

Lucy Wieneke

To order additional copies of this book, contact:
Xlibris Corporation
1-888-795-4274
www.Xlibris.com
Orders@Xlibris.com
29969

CONTENTS

1

The Beginning

A funny thing happened to me on my way to Dodger Stadium—I stayed for 36 years. This is the story of those years, all the laughter, sorrow, anger, and love, as well as the destruction of the extended Dodger family. There is also love for the game of baseball before it became a business.

The first day I worked at the stadium is like running a movie through my mind. The actors are the concession workers shivering in a remote parking lot, waiting to be picked up by the open-air shuttles that would take them up the hill to the stadium. The parking lot is full of people, almost all of whom I would come to know well over the next three decades. Some, in fact, would be my friends forever.

Many of the workers in that parking lot had worked for the Dodgers at the Los Angeles Coliseum, where the team played for its first three seasons in L.A. while waiting for the new stadium to be built in Chavez Ravine. Roy Campanella had his tribute at the Coliseum, and for my birthday in 1959, my husband Tom gave me a ticket to a World Series game against the Chicago White

Sox there. Little did I know sitting there watching the vendors going up and down the steps that I would soon be working with these people and continue working with them until 1997.

It was only seven o'clock in the morning when we climbed on the shuttle and started up the hill. There was a mist that hung around the stadium on the hill, creating a beautiful yet eerie scene. We rode past bushes, trees, ground covering, and even huge cement champagne glasses spilling flowers. As the shuttle rattled along, we drew closer and closer to the magnificent new stadium. I was both excited and scared, having had only a small taste of the type of work I was about to do.

Along with numerous other potential Dodger Stadium employees, I had been sent for a trial run the previous week at the Los Angeles Sports Arena. The same concession company, Arthur Foods, also ran the concessions at the Coliseum and the Sports Arena, where the Lakers played at the time. I was stationed in a small make-shift stand behind the seats on the ground floor. The hot dogs were already cooked, the Coke cups were out, and the stock was ready. Everything went smoothly until half-time when I heard what sounded like a thundering herd of buffalo.

"What's that?" I asked.

The manager laughingly answered, "You'll find out."

Looking around, I saw about a hundred people in front of me. I started to wait on them, one person after another, but the line never seemed to end. I whirled, twirled, and poured so fast it made me dizzy. Then, suddenly the line was gone. There was complete silence. The thundering herd of buffalo had returned to their seats.

It was exciting. Amazingly, I liked it. And not only did I find the work stimulating, but the pay was good, too—$12 a shift!

The shuttle continued up the hill toward the stadium, and I wondered what this day held in store. It was one of the most anticipated days in Los Angeles history: Opening Day at Dodger Stadium, April 10, 1962.

We reported to Arthur Foods concessions on the press entrance level. It was very busy, with hundreds of people milling around tables staffed with supervisors. My badge was issued, and I was told to report to Stand 17 on what was then the Green Level. No one knew where they were going, and I got lost twice before I found Stand 17, which as it turned out was located almost directly below the check-in spot. (I was never good at directions.) The manager greeted me with a grimace.

"Hurry up," she yelled. "We have lots to do."

Everyone was already working—hot dogs were cooking, cups put out, ice poured into bins, peanuts and popcorn and candy put within reach of the cashiers.

We continued with the preparations until zero hour. I took my position as a cashier. Our stand faced the parking lot and was relatively small. There were four cashiers, including me, and in addition to taking money, we would pour Cokes and fill the carry-outs with the food ordered by the customers. The cry finally went out, "The gates are open!"

If I thought there was a herd of buffalo at the Sports Arena, what was this running toward us now? Immediately, there were four lines, one in front of each cashier. The lines went all the way back to the fence, approximately 50 feet away, and they *never* got smaller. The opening ceremonies were conducted, the National Anthem sung, the game started, one inning after another was played, and the game ended—and we stood in one spot getting Cokes, hot dogs, peanuts, etc., as well as taking money and giving change. I was clumsy at first, but out of necessity began to get the hang of selling quickly and what seemed like endlessly.

We knew nothing of what was going on outside, except that people were constantly asking us where the water fountains were. Or they went straight to the accusation, "You didn't put in water fountains because you want us to drink your Cokes!" The reality was that in all the planning and development of arguably the most beautiful baseball stadium of the era, water fountains had been overlooked. Of course, the fans found it hard to believe it was an honest mistake and not a deliberate ploy. I had no way of knowing for sure, but one thing I did know—the people working in the concession stands were not to blame.

It was a horrible day, and I was like a robot. Some people yelled at me, "Move this line!" I finally became so frustrated that I yelled back, "I'll be happy to. Where would you like me to move it?" At one point, my hand went up, "Time out," I announced. "I really need to wipe off my glasses." They were covered with grease.

Some of the customers were nice, and some were funny. Then there were the nasty ones that we learned to spot really fast. They were looking for trouble and just wanted to let out their rage on us. If they'd only known how the place was going to be run 30 years later, they would not have been so critical.

All in all, it was one of the longest days of my life. When it was finally over and the last person had left, we heard these dreadful words, "Let's clean up this mess." We stared in disbelief. Broken and squished hot dogs were lying in dirty wrappers inside boxes stacked to the ceiling, and drink cups sat on the counter made sticky by innumerable Coke spills. Grease was layered on everything, especially us.

"Welcome to Dodger Stadium," I moaned.

The next day, the Los Angeles newspaper headlines read, "Where Are the Water Fountains in Dodger Stadium?"

Despite all the frustrations of the first day—the unrelenting lines, constant activity, demanding and sometimes cranky customers, and the dirt and grease and grime—I liked my new job. The main reason was that I was able to work with people, and I found the interactions fascinating. It was a fascination that did not go away in 36 years.

We created a family at Dodger Stadium. Friendships made that first day lasted for years, sometimes for decades. Among the good friends I made in those early days were Walter and Edna. Edna passed away a few years ago, but Walter and I still keep in touch more than 40 years later. Donna remains one of my good friends, and even though I don't get around as much as I used to, we still make an effort to get together from time to time. As I say, we were a family, and when we see each other even if it's years apart, we have a bond that lasts a lifetime.

I remember the office staff as knowledgeable and competent, but also caring. They were like part of our family as well. Mr. Athern managed the concessions at Dodger Statium for Arthur Foods, and he treated the concession workers respectfully, understanding that by working with us and investing in us as people, we would produce for him. And we did. We worked very hard selling simple but good food at Dodger Stadium using simple cooking areas and a simple method for collecting and tabulating the money. Sometimes, simple is best, especially when it came to this type of operation. Mr. Athern seemed to recognize this. The Dodgers were the beneficiaries of this relationship but so were we as employees. Another example of a smart person who knew how to treat people was Mrs. Johnson, the scheduler. We could always count on her to make the adjustments necessary to keep peace in our part of the Dodger family. The day she left Dodger Stadium was a tragedy.

Mr. Athern and Mrs. Johnson worked in offices at the check-in area between the reserved section and top level, between what was known at the time as the Green and Blue Levels. This is also where the players and announcers checked in, as all the employees of the organization came to work at about the same time. I enjoyed the symbolism of that experience. I also enjoyed riding in the elevator carrying my inventory sheet and cash drawer with Vin Scully, who was always dressed very stylishly and had a warm smile for everyone. Another nice man was Frank Howard, who was the biggest man I ever saw. Standing 6'9" tall with shoulders as broad as the stadium itself, he seemed to fill up the elevator. No one could hit a baseball harder than that man.

Among the workers who showed up around 4:00 p.m. for a night game at the stadium check-in area were the ushers and ticket-takers. My husband Tom, who passed away in 1990, became the ticker-taker at the Stadium Club, where the season ticker-holders sat. He was perfect for that assignment with his professional demeanor and attention to detail. Eventually, when Anaheim Stadium was built, he would become the operations manager there. In the meantime, we made the 25-mile trip from Monrovia in the San Gabriel Valley to Dodger Stadium, where both the Dodgers and Angels played at the time, every day during the summer of 1962.

All in all, we loved being part of the Dodger family. I still can't believe that my 36 years there went as fast as it did.

2

The Dodgers

I was 35 years old when I started working for Arthur Foods and did not drive. It was easier to get around Los Angeles in those days. Our three boys—Stephen, David and Bryant—would often come with us and run downstairs to watch batting practice. The players, ushers, and grounds-keepers were always very nice to them, allowing them to keep many of the home run balls hit during batting practice. They were good players anyway, but they became very popular in the neighborhood when they brought real major league baseballs to the field for over-the-line games.

My mother helped me take care of the boys as she and my dad lived upstairs in a separate apartment for many years. My nationality is French Canadian, though I was born in southern California and have never lived anywhere else. When I started working at Dodger Stadium, we lived in Monrovia in the San Gabriel Valley east of Los Angeles about 25 miles from the stadium. As I say, my husband, Tom, worked at the stadium as an usher and ticket-taker for many years, and my sons

Stephen and David both worked at the Stadium at different times. But back when they were only boys, they would come to a game with wide eyes and stand with me in the hallway of the press entrance where the ball players came out after the game. We'd see Sandy Koufax, Don Drysdale, Maury Wills, and others walking out.

The Dodgers are one of the great historical teams in baseball. They started in Brooklyn in 1883 and moved to Los Angeles in 1958, where the name of the team was shortened from the New York term "Trolley Dodgers" to simply "Dodgers". By the time they moved, all-time greats such as Jackie Robinson, Duke Snider, Gil Hodges, Roy Campanella, Pee Wee Reese, and many others had played for the team.

Walter O'Malley bought a majority ownership in the team in 1950 and had a vision for the Dodgers to move. He began looking for a location to build a stadium in the West, eventually deciding on a picturesque spot overlooking downtown Los Angeles known as Chavez Ravine. The team moved before the stadium was completed, however, and the new L.A. Dodgers played in the Los Angeles Memorial Coliseum for several years. The Coliseum had not been built for baseball, and the result was a 250-foot left field fence with a screen the size of a circus tent hung up to keep the balls in the park. This feature is what led to the famous "Moon Shots" from left-handed hitter Wally Moon, who shaped his swing to take advantage of the short porch in left field.

Amazingly, the Dodgers won the National League pennant in 1959 playing on this field. They faced the Chicago White Sox who brought in slugger Ted Kluszewski and household names like Luis Aparicio and Nellie Fox against the Dodgers. While there were future Hall of Famers Gil Hodges and Duke Snider on the team, there were also many new stars such as Maury Wills, Jim Gilliam, John Roseboro, Norm Larker, and Don Demeter to add to the stellar pitching of Sandy Koufax, Don Drysdale, and Johnny Podres. The Dodgers won the World Series in six games, and Larry Sherry was the Most Valuable Player.

The Dodgers were a California team with a tremendous fan following by the time they moved to Dodger Stadium in 1962. The stadium itself was a perfect symbol of California with palm trees visible behind the outfield fences and a gentle breeze blowing through the distant hills. It was an ideal setting for baseball, and the Dodgers put an exciting team on the field in the 1960s.

Sandy Koufax was my favorite. Over the years I watched every game he pitched at the stadium. He was a beautiful thing to watch when he was pitching; come to think of it, he was a beautiful thing to watch when he wasn't pitching. The night he pitched his perfect game in 1965, I was working right behind home plate on the yellow level. It was so exciting toward the end of the game that everyone seemed to be holding their breath.

When the last pitch went across the plate—*strike!*—the stadium exploded. The catcher John Roseboro ran to Sandy, jumped up, wrapped himself around him, and they hugged. I was literally jumping up and down and yelling, too. A beautiful thing to watch.

Later, I was working in the pavilion, and I was visiting with another female worker when Tommy, the grounds-keeper, came up to us and said, "Lucy, Sandy is in the bull pen." My friend and I walked by, and there was Sandy, crouching and catching for a young pitcher. I looked at him and before I knew what I was doing blurted out, "You're beautiful."

My friend looked at me and said, "I can't believe you did that."

Me either. I'm blushing now, but not at the time!

I also recall one day in batting practice before the game. Don Drysdale, who was very proud of his hitting as well as his pitching, was throwing. One of our employees was sitting in a seat waiting for the stand to open and yelled, "Hey, Drysdale, Koufax is hitting better than you." All of us around heard Don yell back, "You're full of crap!" And Don was right.

The player who was the most fun over the years had to be another Don, however—Don Sutton. I was stationed in the left field pavilion, and Don liked to come over to the stand during batting practice. "I'm hiding out from Tommy," he'd say, referring to Manager Tommy LaSorda. If there was anything Don loved, it was popping champagne corks. It is wasn't somebody's birthday, it was some other occasion like when he got his flying license. The concession workers brought the food, and Don brought the champagne. He didn't drink it—I think he just liked to open the bottles and pop the corks. His wife and children joined us a couple of times. On my birthday, I was smashed before the gates ever opened. I had to drink coffee to get myself together. The next day, Tommy the grounds-keeper brought wine—same thing. Don looked at me and said, "Lucy, are you smashed again?" (I hasten to add I rarely got smashed while on the job.)

It was also the time of gas rationing. One day, I mentioned to Don that I needed gas. He answered quickly, "Tommy's always got plenty of gas. You could get some from him."

Don would come into the stand and dump ice in the bins to the delight of the fans. He would wait on the customers in his uniform, sign autographs, and just be a great guy. Some of my favorite memories are of being in the pavilion and knowing Don Sutton.

I have lots of pictures and balls signed by him, but my favorite souvenir is a signed champagne bottle.

While in the pavilion, we became acquainted with the Little Old Lady from Pasadena. Literally. Her name was Francis, she lived in Pasadena, and she drove her car fast. She came to every game and sat in the pavilion. All the players knew her because she would stand at the railing and yell at them. If one of the Dodgers hit a home run, she would ring her cowbell, jump up and down, and scream wildly. We allowed her into our parties. One Sunday morning, we were set up, and it began to pour down rain. It was coming down in torrents. The sight I will never forget is Francis in the pavilion at the rail in the torrential ran screaming at the top of her lungs, "Play ball!"

My favorite thing to do in the pavilion was to get two or three batting practice home run balls and save them until the fans started coming in. Then I'd pull a kid aside and say, "Look, I think you're just the right boy (or girl) for this ball." Their eyes would open wide, and the smile was pure joy. I just loved doing that.

I was having a ball, if you'll excuse the pun. The people in the office didn't think it was so great, however. There was not much for them to do about it until the manager from Stand 18, way up on what's now the blue level, quit. Mr. Atherne, our very capable boss, decided it was time for Lucy to have a BIG stand and stop having the time of everyone's life. The honeymoon was over.

I said goodbye to Don and sadly made my way upstairs to the biggest and scariest stand I'd ever seen. It turned out nicely for Don Sutton, though. An African-American woman named Joan took over in the pavilion, and she and her husband became friends with Don. He seemed to be in hog heaven because Joan cooked grits, black-eyed peas, and other Southern food that reminded him of his birthplace—Clio, Alabama.

As for me, I was not in hog heaven or any other kind of heaven. I was scared to death of this humongous new place with at least 18 people working in it. Walking from one end to the other was an ordeal. It was a double stand in cafeteria style. Fan would come in through the center and go down either side, picking up their food and drinks. There were four cashiers, two on each end, two bartenders inside, and two separate bars on the outside of the cashiers. Managing this complex an operation was a huge task. The first few weeks, I was so tired I would fall into bed as soon as I got home. I also cried a lot. Mr. Atherne would not hear my pleas for another stand. When I asked him why, he said, "Because I know you can do it, Lucille."

I decided it was sink or swim. When I finally stopped fighting it, I was all right. Mr. Atherne was right—I could do it. Over time, I learned to love the stand and my crew.

The stand became a well-oiled machine. It was an efficient operation, and the fans picked up their food and drink without waiting on a normal night. Of course, some nights were not normal and it was impossible to keep up with the demand, but we worked together and did the best we could.

Meanwhile, the Dodgers were thriving in their new stadium. In their first season of 1962, they won the pennant with 102 victories. Maury Wills stole a record 104 bases, and Tommy Davis won the batting crown and knocked in 153 runs. As for the pitchers, Don Drysdale won the Cy Young Award in the National League, and Sandy Koufax led the league in ERA. The Dodgers won the pennant again in 1963 and this time swept the New York Yankees in the World Series. Sandy Koufax was unbelievable with a 25-5 record, 1.88 ERA, and 306 strikeouts. He won everything that year: Most Valuable Player, Cy Young award, and MVP of the World Series. The Dodgers also beat the Yankees in the 1965 World Series and won the NL pennant again in 1966, losing to the Baltimore Orioles in the World Series.

With the retirements of Koufax, Drysdale, and other mainstays of the 1960s, the success of the 1970s was a pleasant surprise and a moving testimony to the Dodger family. Peter O'Malley took over from his father Walter in 1970 and built an impressive team that won three pennants, though no World Series, and had 910 victories. The infield combination of Steve Garvey, Davey Lopes, Bill Russell, and Ron Cey played together for almost the entire decade, and Walter Alston retired in favor of the energetic and outspoken Tommy LaSorda in 1977. There were many fine pitchers, though none could compare to Koufax and Drysdale. Among them was Tommy John, whose arm was rebuilt by Dr. Frank Jobe. The best of the decade was a man named Don Sutton, who won 21 games in 1976 and a total of 21 in the 1970s.

3

People in the Stands

My memories of the concession stands at Dodger Stadium are a mixture of fun and sadness. One day, a young Mexican woman came to work for me. She was so small, I wondered if she would make it there. She promptly took over the condiments. She got a stool, climbed up and filled the big metal containers. She take them down and wash them later. Never complaining, she won my heart. I affectionately nicknamed her Peanut, and as long as I was at the stadium, everyone called her by that name. She had her third child—a boy after two girls—while working with me, and we gave her a big shower in the stadium.

The reason I mention everyone's nationality is to show how all of us from different cultures and backgrounds became a family. At the time I came to work in Stand 18, there was George, who is Hispanic and worked on the outside bar connected with the stand. He was like the bartender at the corner bar—we'd all talk over our problems with him.

Serving nachos at the end of the counter was my little Ana, who is Hispanic and very sweet. She was raising two girls alone and had two jobs. I'm happy to report that after a few years, Ana and George fell in love. They went on to buy a video store together in La Puente called "Mexicana Video".

On the grill was Albert, who is Jewish and had worked at the Sheriff's Department before retiring. He worked hard on that grill, and it was HOT. He was funny, too. For some reason, he wore a clown nose and hair one day into the stand. Without hesitation, I said, "Come with me." We went up to the office and asked for Mr. Atherne. When he came out, I said, "Some clown wants to see you." He looked at Al and shook his head. "Oh, Lucy," he muttered. By that time, Mr. A. knew me and smiled.

Next on the grill were Rene, whom I will tell you about soon, and Charles, a husky African-American who was probably the neatest man I've ever met, very careful in everything he did. How he could stand it at that messy, smelly hot dog grill night after night, I'll never know.

Mike was on fries. He was the opposite of Charles with mashed fries everywhere—on the counters, on our shoes, in our hair. He did cook some good fries, though. He's Jewish and was a teacher for many years, perhaps still is. Mike was also a movie buff, and he and I would discuss movies all the time. I also yelled at Mike more than anyone else. He loved to watch me explode, so he would "detonate" me on a regular basis. Later, with

Marriott, I yelled at Mike and was not kind. I regret that. I wasn't very kind to anyone then, least of all myself, but I'll tell that story in its place.

Next we come to the Italian Connection: Rose and Irma. They poured Cokes on the far end and liked their made-up name. Rose was from New Jersey, and Irma from Sicily. Their accents were a little hard to understand, but they both expressed themselves with their hands as well as their speech. They were very funny and loved being with people. I don't know who had more fun—them or their customers—and they were the fastest drink pourers I've ever seen.

On the nachos was Cookie, a very attractive African-American woman with a great sense of humor.

Then there was Yolanda. She's Hispanic and had such an upbeat disposition that we sometimes called her "sunshine". She also loved to talk and no idea of time when she was talking to someone. Many times I had to retrieve her from a conversation and bring her back to the stand. She was bubbly and always seemed to be laughing, but one day the laughter stopped for her. I was watching TV at home and heard this awful story on the news about a young girl in high school who was getting off the school bus and was hit and killed by a 16-year-old driving without a driver's license. I had a funny feeling about it when the phone rang. It was a fellow worker.

"Did you hear about Yolanda's daughter?" she asked.

I dropped the phone. The relationship between her and her daughter was very close. I tried to get Yolanda on the phone, but it was busy. I went back to watching the TV with tears running down my face. The phone rang again. I answered and this time heard, "Lucy, I lost my Rhonda." I could barely understand her, she was crying so hard.

We took up a collection at the stadium. Everyone was broken-hearted over the tragedy. They showed the kids from the high school on TV, and the community came together to support Yolanda. It broke my heart to watch Yolanda and her husband on TV going into the church for the funeral. We didn't know if she would ever recover. She called me one day shortly after the funeral. She knew how I felt about life after death. We talked about the Light and things that cannot be explained. Then she said she had a story to tell me. She said that a few days after Rhonda's death, she heard a strange noise at the screen door. It was a meowing sound. She looked, and there on the other side of the screen was a small white kitten. It was a tight-knot community, and everyone knew everyone else's pet, but she had never seen this kitten before. She opened the door. The kitten ran into the house, passed Yolanda, and went into Rhonda's bedroom, where it jumped on the bed and sat there looking at her.

When her son came home, he couldn't believe it, but the kitten would rub up against them both and purr. It also went next door to visit the aunt's house, then came back. I had goose flesh when Yolanda told me.

"You know that's your daughter coming back to comfort you," I said. "She won't stay long."

"I know that, Lucy."

Sure enough, in three days, the kitten disappeared. A really strange part was that Rhonda's birthday had been coming up, and she had told Yolanda she wanted blue contact lenses. This kitten had beautiful blue eyes.

I love telling that story. It took quite a long time for Yolanda's laughter to return. While she eventually got her sunshine back, there is a sadness deep inside that of course never goes away. I know she feels as if she had a very special spiritual experience, and I believe she did, too.

Now back to my stand. On the outside bar was Sheila. She was very sharp, funny, pretty African-American woman. I think she made more tips than anyone else in the stadium because she was so attentive to the customers. The cashier on the end was Ophelia, a lovely older Hispanic lady who happened to be the mother of one of the future Marriott supervisors.

Henny worked as cashier also and is was one of my regular workers for almost 20 years. She is probably the funniest woman I've ever known. She's Danish with a thick accent and brutally truthful, full of zest and snappy answers. If you don't want an answer, don't ask Henny. But she says things in such a funny way that it makes you laugh. I could hear her wonderful Danish accent mumbling under her breath. She always mumbled to herself. If she didn't like something, she'd yell, "This is da pits!" We'd double over laughing. Henny quite right after I did. I told her, "I love you, I can't help it."

Henny had a wonderful green-and-yellow parrot named Mambo. When I called her, I could hear him laughing every time she did, and it sounded just like her. One time, Henny was going to Denmark and left Mambo with me. I had a great time singing with the bird, taking him to the highest notes possible. He would tilt his head back and emit this strange, shrill sound. Meanwhile, my sister Ann was visiting, and she was teasing him in a variety of creative ways. By the time Henny came back, the poor bird was a basket case. Henny took Mambo from the cage, and the tortured bird bit her finger. She screamed in pain until she could finally get his beak off her finger. She yelled at us in her thick Danish accent, "What have you done to my bird?" The last sight I remember is Mambo going crazy in his cage as she put him in her car. She informed us that it took her six months to calm him down.

Cashiering on the other end was Donna. She was my assistant manager and my friend. She's loyal, kind, honest, funny, and smart, and a dozen other things that are all good. She is also a great worker. Donna was raised on a farm in Iowa. I've noticed that people raised on farms are sometimes put together better than the rest of us. Donna and I rode in together for years and have had many laughs, cries, disappointments, and surprises together. We spent a lot of time at our favorite restaurant on Sunset Boulevard, Taix. We'd go if it was a day game and have dinner. Donna lost her husband while working at the stadium, and I lost mine too, sometime later—a sad time.

Sometimes Gayle cashiered on the same end as Donna. She also filled in other places. Gayle was one of our best workers. She's African-American and always did things without a fuss. She had a medical problem but never complained. On the other hand, I complained a lot! I felt guilty about that, and later I felt guilty about other things I did under stress.

I must mention Pat, who came into the stand after Ana left. When she first came to Stand 18, she was very pregnant. We were afraid she'd have the baby while serving nachos but managed to hold out until she was in a more appropriate setting. Later, I'm afraid Pat also received some of my wrath after Arthur Foods left the stadium and things changed so much. I hope she'll forgive me, too!

On the inside bar was Kay, whom I adored. He was of German heritage and probably the funniest man I've ever known. He bartended next to me because he made me laugh so much. Kay was a hypochondriac, and he was always going to faint or had a pain he couldn't figure out, or some other health crisis. He had been in show business, a dancer on stage mostly, so he was very dramatic about everything. He would sometimes get sneezing attacks, and when it was coming on, he'd say, "Oh no, oh no." He would get in a corner and brace himself against a wall because the sneezing hurt his back so badly. The sneezes would begin and shake him from head to foot. He kept muttering, "oh no, oh no." I know it sounds cruel, but I couldn't help laughing at him. One day, he decided to test the people in line. He took a big black plastic rat that we just happened to have (that's another story), and put it in his smock with the head sticking out. "Let's see how long before someone says something," he said. The fans filed through. They'd look at Kay, order a beer, then look away. This went on for quite a while. Finally, a young woman came up, ordered her beer, and said, "By the way, you need a new exterminator." Kay yelled, "There you go—the beer's on me!" He had a very high I.Q. and would answer almost every question when we played Trivial Pursuit. When I knew an answer, I'd say it in the middle of the question because that was the only way to beat Kay.

God rest Kay's soul, he died a number of years ago now. He knew he was dying, so he went on a cruise and died in his sleep on the ship. That's Kay for you.

Another sad memory is of Rene, who worked for me a long time in Stand 18. He was a nice young man but stubborn as a mule. He'd turn purple before doing what I asked. I'd send him away to another stand, but he'd always charm his way back. Sometimes, he'd cook, but mostly he ran a line.

Rene was married and had a lovely wife, Selma, and two little boys. While working the third years with Marriott, Rene began to feel ill. When he finally went to the doctor, they found he had a genetic disease inherited from his father. It was too late to do anything about it.

We were all devastated. We took up a collection in the stadium concessions, and ushers put posters up and handed out flyers to the other workers. Albert, who worked the grill cooking hamburgers, had worked for me forever and was a father figure to Rene and others in the stand, stood and handed out the flyers. When the Marriott supervisors told him it was against the rules, Al said, "Go fry your ears," and kept on.

We got the thousand dollars we were shooting for. The G.M. had given Rene all the tickers he wanted to the games and was very good to him. We had a party in the stand, and Selma and the boys came. Mike, one of our regular workers, made a big banner that said, "Beat the odds, Rene!" We gave them the money, and the ushers came up and gave him cards and money. We all took separate pictures with Rene, and I let him wait on about four customers. He was very frail by this time. They found traces of the disease in the boys, but Selma is a very strong person. She has put herself through paramedic school and got a job with the Fire

Department. After Rene's death, Selma told me Rene thought of me as his mom. He died at the age of 31.

When Pope John Paul II came to Dodger Stadium, we had to go through metal detectors to get into the stadium. The security was the tightest I've ever seen. We could see at least six FBI agents on every level. There was a rehearsal way before the event with choirs and other singers. The singer from "Les Miserables" was there and rehearsing a song he performed in the musical. He had a marvelous voice.

The field looked beautiful—flowers, a huge white cross, red carpets. It was filled with hundreds of Cardinals, monsignors, priests, and nuns. The program began, and the performer from "Les Miserables" came out to sing. The moment he opened his mouth, the helicopter carrying the Pope appeared and kept circling around the stadium. No one could hear a word. The helicopter landed just as the poor man stopped singing. He shrugged his shoulders and walked away. What else could he do?

At least I heard him in rehearsal!

It was always forbidden to make betting pools in the stadium. It has also gone on since Opening Day in 1962 and will continue until the stadium closes its gates. You get ten malt spoons and write out 1 to 10 on them, then put them in a cup. Each person pays an amount to enter and picks a spoon. The winner has the number that's the combined score of the two teams at the end of the game.

One day, right after Mr. Atherne had issued a directive to each stand saying absolutely no pools, a new worker was on the elevator. He pulled out his malt spoon and show it to the man standing next to him. "Ain't that a hell of a number to get in the pool?" he asked. You guessed it—the man next to him was Mr. Atherne.

I can still see Tommy LaSorda when he was trying to lose weight, running around the field during batting practice. On a very hot day, he was really puffing, but on he went. Looking down from the stands, some of us yelled, "Way to go, Tommy!" He gave us the thumbs up. We were glad—when he raised his hand, we weren't sure which sign we would get.

I really must write about Ricky. He is one of my fondest memories. He came to us in Stand 18 one day in 1984. He's African-American and has the most beautiful smile I've ever seen. Every time I came near him, he would shy away. Finally, I said, "Ricky, I'm really not going to hit you." He was a great worker and finally must have realized we were on his side. Everyone in the stand adored Ricky. It seems he had lost his wife some time earlier, and after that, he just didn't care. He did have two wonderful sons. But apparently he couldn't handle the loss and got into drugs. We tried to protect Ricky and at the end of the season got together to buy him a watch. We made a big fuss, but we were all aware that the watch could very well go for drugs that night. We didn't care. It was the gesture that counted.

We began to cover for him around supervisors, but one day a big-wig saw him. We all pleaded with him and signed a petition, but to no avail. I'll always remember that wonderful smile when we presented Ricky with that watch. God bless him, wherever he is.

While in Stand 18, we were given heavy polyester smocks to wear for uniforms. They felt like overcoats. The temperature in the stand was something like 100 degrees with the grills, fryers, and motors going. It was the middle of summer. It was outrageous, but the other workers kept telling me that you can't fight City Hall. "We'll see," was my answer. I decided that the next day, we'd all take our smocks off. I discussed this idea with another manager who was something of a rebel. He agreed to do the same in his stand.

The rebellion was on. One of the supervisors came by and ordered us to put our smocks back on. "You can't do this!" he shouted.

"Oh yes, we can," I replied. "We're burning up."

"Tell them to put those smocks on!"

"If they do, I'm sending them all to First Air because they're all sick from the heat."

He threw up his hands and walked out. The next day, when we came into work, they gave us all little white aprons instead of the polyester smocks. I threw one up in the air and yelled, "Yippee!" My son David, who worked with me at the time, said, "Way to go, Mom." When I went into my stand, the whole crew stood up and applauded. That was a great moment. I've always thought you could fight City Hall, and it helped that the Arthur Foods people were decent people and did not want to see us suffer.

I also wrote a newsletter for a few years. It was done in a tongue-in-cheek manner, to make our gripes known in a funny way. I'd lay one on each of the desks in the office. It was fun, and they never minded. They would all laugh about it.

We had a policy in the stand that we would be pleasant to customers who brought food back. We'd replace it instantly. If it was a hot dog, we'd give them a double dog to replace the one they returned. Why should you argue with your customers? They came to have a good time, not to fight with someone. It's such an easy concept, but some managers never understood it. They would fight as hard as if it they had to buy the replacement item with their own money.

This reminds me of a time before I was managing when we had a manager there who loved to argue with customers. One night, a man came back with his popcorn.

The man very politely said, "This popcorn isn't hot. Could I get another one?"

"What do you mean, it isn't hot?" the manager said accusingly. "It just came out of the machine."

This was a lie because I had seen the manager put the popcorn in the case right before it was purchased. It could not possible have gotten hot in that short time.

"Well, I can't help that," the customer persisted. "It just isn't hot."

"I just can't understand why it isn't hot," the manager replied. "You know, we just can't replace every item customers bring back."

"Listen, I didn't come here to argue. I came here ot watch the game," the man said wearily.

I couldn't stand it any longer. I took the box of popcorn from the man and gave him another box.

"There you go, sir," I said pleasantly. "Have a nice evening." Then I looked at the stupid manager and said, "Why would you do that?"

He didn't answer. He was undoubtedly the rudest man I've ever know and took delight in ruining someone's day. He didn't get away with it that time, though!

We had regular customers who would come to the stand almost every game. One beautiful gal named Susie was one of them. For one of my birthdays, she made me a cake shaped like a baseball glove with a ball in the center. She ended up marrying the former Dodger player and manager, Bill Russell, and we were all very happy for her.

For most of my 36 years at Dodger Stadium, we loved to laugh and play jokes. One of my favorites was to pick someone in my line on a busy night. You know the type—fidgeting first on one foot then the other, looking around, sighing impatiently. He would keep getting closer and closer to the front as I served the customers ahead of him. Finally, after waiting for all the other customers to get served, he'd reach the front of the line. Before he opened his mouth to order, I'd say, "Sorry, sir, I have to close this line."

Before he had a fit, I'd quickly laugh and say, "Just kidding!" The people in the other lines would get the joke, and the customer would always end up laughing as well.

If I'm counting right, I heard the National Anthem about 4,000 times. But I never get tired of it. And there was also something special about the stadium when she was all dressed up for a World Series. The flags would be draped over the lower deck, and the field would be perfectly manicured. You could feel the excitement in the air, and before long, the fans would be screaming and jumping, and every single seat would be filled. It was quite a spectacle.

As I've said, there were many spectacles during my time at Dodger Stadium. For many years, while Arthur Foods ran the concessions, the workers came together as a family at the stadium and we learned to love each other. We thought it would never end.

But we were wrong.

Lucy Wieneke, Author

Break Time

Donna and Lucy

Five All Stars

Food & Soft Drinks Only

I survived 91!

Lucy (7th from left), & others on the field

Lucy and Don Sutton

Lucy with Son Steve

Lucy, Husband Tom, Mother Maria

Lucy's Son Bryant & his wife Elvira

Lucy's Son Dave

Part of the Family

The Crew

4

Celebrities

I have always been fascinated with Hollywood, dating from the days when I was in my late teens and lived with my mom, dad, two brothers, and three sisters in a small house on Olympic and Valencia near downtown Los Angeles. I would take the bus into Hollywood, often alone, and eventually began to visit the radio station KFUD at Third and Vermont. It soon became a regular spot for me, and I even had a secretarial job at the station for a while, which is odd only because I didn't know how to type. There were two announcers at the station, Clyde Cadwell and Fred Allison, who liked having me around so much that they did almost all of my typing.

I also became friends with Cliffy Stone, who is now in the Country Western Hall of Fame, and the comedian Stan Freeberg, who enjoyed doing impersonations. One I still remember was his imitation of FDR when he said, "I hate war, Eleanor hates war, and I hate Eleanor." FDR is one of my heroes, but Stan could make anything funny. He later become Beanie the Seasick Sea Serpent on T.V.

During this period, I was writing song lyrics and having some success with them when one day I heard my lyrics in a song on the radio. I was upset and ended up suing the people who made the record, but winning the lawsuit ruined any career I might have had in the music business. No one would have anything to do with my lyrics after that.

I brought this history and a longstanding fascination with Hollywood to the concession stand. Along with others, I was always on the lookout for movie stars. I remember a game in 1965 when I looked up to see Bob Hope standing in front of me. He was at the peak of his popularity then, but he was very nice and spent time talking to me and the kid who was cooking hot dogs. He cracked a couple of jokes, after which he asked the kid, "So, do you listen to my show?"

The smart-mouth kid answered, "No, I always turn you off."

I gulped and wondered how to get out of this. Then I said, "Mr. Hope, did you know that stupidity is a requirement for working here?"

He stared at me and finally smiled.

At another game, I saw Omar Sharif waiting several people back in my line. When he reached the front, I heard his wonderful deep voice, "May I have a cup of coffee?"

"Of course, Mr. Sharif," I purred.

"Thank you, my dear," he said as I gave him his coffee. He left me a nickle tip.

Walter Matthau was another big Dodger fan. We were in the pavilion one night for Hollywood Stars night, and he came through throwing a Frisbee. He threw it to us, but all he really needed to do was look at us to make us laugh. He was a funny man.

As I mentioned earlier, my husband Tom was the ticker-taker at the Stadium Club, and he frequently encountered celebrities there. There is no doubt, however, about his most memorable experience there. One night, he came by with a big grin on his face.

"What are you smiling about?" I asked. "You look like the cat who swallowed the canary."

"Better than that," he said mysteriously.

"What is it?"

Smiling even more broadly, he said, "I got kissed by Marilyn Monroe tonight."

"Yeah, sure," I replied. "And I got asked out by Frank Sinatra."

"No kidding," he insisted. "She was on the field before the game and got introduced to the fans. They put me in charge of taking her onto the field and bringing her back. After it was over, she reached up, gave me a big kiss, and said, "'Thank you, sweetie.'"

I worked different stands over the years and also managed in several locations. One year, I managed the Club Stand by the press box. Kato, the chef, would bring these sumptuous trays by on his way to Mr. O'Malley's box, picking up any items they needed from us. Sometimes, he'd bring us strawberries and other goodies.

We had to be careful on the Club Level and cater to everyone. We never knew if a customer was a player's mother, wife, or relative, or some other famous person. It was very quiet and not very busy. It was an entirely different atmosphere from the other noisy, busy stands.

I remember Jack Benny coming up one day and asking how much the cigars were. They were only ten cents apiece, but he did not buy one.

We had a thrill one day when Cary Grant came up during the game. His daughter and her governess were with him. Cary said, as only he could, "Hello, doll. How about some ice cream?"

Rosalind Russell was also a great fan, always on the Club Level. Another of my favorite people to see there was Vin Scully. He's such a lovely man, so down-to-earth, and arguably the greatest announcer of all time.

5

Special Events

Most of us who worked at the stadium also worked at the Los Angeles Coliseum and the Los Angeles Sports Arena, where Arthur Foods also had the concessions contract. The Coliseum was especially interesting because the concession stands were built right up under the stands where the fans sat in concrete alcoves. The store rooms had no lights and were just cut-outs in the cement wall. We always went into the store room very carefully and came out fast if we saw too yellow eyes in there!

One event at the Coliseum was a major boxing match, and our portable stand was located in the center of the field near the ring. The field was packed with people, and I'm sure no one was admitted without a bottle of booze. Our stand was lit up like a Christmas tree in the middle of this wild atmosphere. Everyone in the seat was yelling, and the more they drank, the louder they yelled. They finally turned their attention to us and apparently thought we were the enemy and our stand was a foxhole. They started throwing their empty bottles at us.

"Hit the dirt!" our manager called as any good sergeant would.

"We lay on the ground and discussed what to do next as the bottles flew over us. Our sergeant—excuse me, manager—said, "Listen, we're in a tough spot, men." Then he added, "Sorry, you too, Lucy." He continued, "We can crawl on our bellies and try to make it to the tunnel, but they might see us."

"Sir?" piped on of the workers on the ground. "Can we turn out the lights and go out in the dark?"

"Good thinking," Sergeant Walter replied.

And that was what we did.

There were numerous concerts at the Sports Arena, and one of the most memorable was a James Brown concert. I thought he was a great performer and had been looking forward to that night, but it turned into a disaster. While we were setting up, we could see out the huge glass panels near the entrance of the arena. The number of people outside the doors was increasingly rapidly. When I looked out a half-hour later, the crowd had grown tremendously, and it kept growing each time I checked. Finally, the doors opened, but the concert had apparently been sold out. We watched from the stands as the ushers yelled, "There are no tickets left!" But these fans wanted in, so they stormed the glass panels. They ran right through them into the arena and right over anyone who fell on the floor. In the stand, we hid under the counters—we may not be brave, but we're not stupid, either.

We also saw our share of celebrities at the Sports Arena. During one afternoon event, Natalie Wood and Robert Wagner stood at our stand and talked with us for an hour. They were absolutely charming and sweet, and I can still remember how young and beautiful they looked. Another night at the Sports Arena, one of USC's most famous alums, John Wayne, was standing next to me in the tunnel, waiting to be introduced at one of the university's events being held there. I was surprised to see that he was wringing his hand nervously, and I realized that even "The Duke" could get butterflies.

The first time I heard the words "Rolling Stones" was downstairs at the Sports Arena. "What's a Rolling Stone?" I asked an usher who was watching me count my stock. "Whatever it is, I hope it doesn't gather any moss."

One thing they certainly had gathered was fans. These were fans who actually stayed in their seats at first, affording us an opportunity to see some of the show. But at one point, we could see the huge crowd moving toward the stage. Every time Mick Jagger would sing, "Hey, you, get offa my cloud!" he would stompt his foot, and the young fans would go nuts. More and more of them massed in the center aisle until there was no longer an aisle, just a huge wave of human flesh shoving ever closer to the performers. It took every police officer and security guard to hold them back, and I honestly thought they would lose the battle. It became easy for me to understand how one of these events could deteriorate into catastrophe. Mick and the other "Stones" must have heaved a sigh of relief when they got off the stage that night.

At the Sports Arena, we worked every kind of event—the Mexican rodeo, fights, dog shows, Scottish Black Watch, ice shows, political rallies, Russian Cossacks, Lippizoner Stallions, basketball games, and many others. For the two nights we worked the Pink Floyd concert, we were all stoned from second-hand marijuana smoke in the building. Honestly, we barely knew where we were or what was going on. Somehow, I felt that was a blessing.

The event I liked best was the International Circus with the Flying Walendas. They took our breath away. I used to stand near them and watch them up above courting death. They were an incredible sight.

During one circus, however, I made the mistake of standing beside the cannon. You don't get many smart points for that. "BOOM!" went the cannon. A man flew out, and my head flew off, or seemed like it. I couldn't hear for hours, and I was shaking a lot longer than that.

At the international circus, they had wonderful clowns. I was working on the floor level, right next to where the clowns had their dressing room. There was one clown who absolutely killed me. He was dressed up as a ridiculous-looking bride with all his clown make-up, a huge dress, a wedding veil, and the great big flat shoes clowns often wear. The clown knew I thought he was funny, and he would come up and dance for me with those crazy shoes of his.

One night, as he was about to perform, he came up and handed me a small cup. "Put a little orange drink in here, would you, honey." I said, "Sure. Let me dump out the water first, though." Before he could say anything, it was done. "What have you done?" he screamed. "That was my vodka. Now I have to go on cold!" By this time, the sight of him with that face and that veil, wearing those shoes, with this distraught look on his face was too much for me. I started laughing so hard that I fell on the floor.

As I say, many of the same people who worked at Dodger Stadium also worked at the LA Coliseum and Sports Arena, bringing us closer together in many ways. These were occasional or seasonal events, however. The core of our relationship was forged at Dodger Stadium, however, where we worked at least 81 games from late spring to the end of summer as well as special events.

Trailer shows were a regular event at Dodger Stadium, and not one of the most popular among the workers. They were often held in November when it was rainy or cold, or both. We had outdoor stands in the parking lots and needed to build shelters from cardboard boxes to keep from freezing. There were big electric everywhere, along with containers of water and coffee. Hot dogs were cooked in big pots stuck in wooden holes with sterno cans underneath. It was as primitive as you can get, and I could never figure out where they got the coffee.

A smiling trailer salesman came up one morning and asked, "How's the coffee?"

"Like melted tar paper," I answered truthfully.

One of the greatest times we had was when the Olympics came to Los Angeles in 1984, and the United States and Japan played baseball at Dodger Stadium. We were all caught up in the pins. I finally had so many that I put them on a white blouse, cut off the sleeves, and wore it over my uniform. I'd leave the stand and immediately be swamped by pin traders. Sometimes, they'd get on their knees to see the pins on the bottom of the blouse. I especially loved the pins from other countries. There was a group of Japanese ladies who came in wearing kimonos, and we traded pins from our home countries.

It impressed me that the Japanese and USA teams were on the field together, all standing at attention with their hands over their hearts while the American National Anthem was played. Forty years earlier, these two nations were fighting a bloody war. It was something to think about.

I kept my pins. It was hard work to get them, and I wanted to enjoy them. Some of the workers were selling them for good money, but where's the fun in that? Money isn't everything.

6

Changes

We started hearing rumors that Arthur Foods was out toward the end of the 1990 season. The rumors were flying that Marriott was going to be the new concession. One morning, before the season began, I called the office. Mr. Atherne answered.

"Is it true?" I asked.

"Yes," he said. "We have to be out tomorrow."

My eyes filled with tears.

"Goodbye, Lucille. Have a good life."

It was the beginning of the end.

All the concession workers received notices from Marriott to come to a meeting in March 1991. There were a lot of speeches that day, and most of them contained the words, "We're going to make this our flagship!" Representatives of the Dodger Office also spoke, saying how wonderful it was going to be. They did serve an excellent lunch.

The next meeting at the stadium was a real doozy. First, they showed us their new stands. Many of them were franchises, not the regular stands serving our usual set of simple items. All the managers followed one of the supervisors. He took us to a small stand, which was tiled and had a new door separating the cooking area from the front of the stand. The kitchen had a very high ceiling. The gentleman showing us around asked, "Do you have any questions?"

"I have one," I replied. "How do you breathe in here?"

He didn't have an answer. We went back to the meeting room where the big bomb was about to drop. The general manager was sitting with the other Marriott big wigs. He informed us that they would have grilled Dodger Dogs in only two stands in the entire stadium. The rest of the stands would have steamed dogs.

We erupted. "You can't do that! The fans will riot."

The general manager smiled and reassured us.

We didn't know at the time that one of the reasons for their decisions was the need to bring the stands up to code. Unfortunately, the new concessions company had apparently spent so much money on its flagship that it didn't have the money to put vents in all the stands.

I chose to work at Carl's Jr. for the freeway series with the Angels. It was located where my old stand used to be. I took my crew with me. It was a whole new ball game, so to speak. There were Carl's Jr. supervisors standing over us like vultures. They second-guessed us at every turn and made our lives in that stand miserable. We had a union contract that we would be the servers, but they didn't seem to like it at all. After two days, I said, "I'm outta here."

I asked for the outside stand facing the parking lot. It was one of the two stands serving grilled hot dogs, and we could breathe up there. My crew came with me, and we said goodbye to Carl's Jr. forever.

Marriott had wisely kept the Arthur Foods scheduling team of Peggy and Barbara. Scheduling is one of the most important jobs in running a big concession operation like ours. Of course, the real issue that was uppermost on all our minds, that we dared not even talk about, was coming fast. Opening Day of the season is always the most hectic and busiest day of the year. It's bad enough when everyone knows what they're doing. What would it be like when no one in charge knew what they were doing?

Each and every concession person dreaded it beyond words. D-Day was here!

We went to the parking lot designated to check in. There were lines everywhere. So many people were running around, it looked like casting for Cleopatra. It was utter chaos. I don't know who looked more confused—the supervisors or the concession workers. There was a line for managers and assistants to go right in. That was the only thing they got right. Donna and I arrived at the stand, and there was one other person there. We knew we were in deep doo-doo. The stock was piled to the ceiling. We tried to count some of it, but much of it was screwed up. That's not what we were worried about. We didn't have a crew! One or two people would come in every hour. We had to get hot dogs cooking, stock out, ice poured, etc. The Clock was ticking! It was like the movie *High Noon*; the only difference was the worse thing that could happen to Gary Cooper was that he'd get killed.

We did the best we could. We had a few hot dogs cooked, and had a couple of cashiers. The gates opened, and I don't know how we got through that day. The fans were irate, but when they saw the mess we were in, they forgave us. They did not forgive Marriott, however!

There's not a person who worked that day who will ever forget it. The next day, the Marriott office staff had shirts printed up that said, "We Survived Opening Day at Dodger Stadium!" They should have printed them up for the fans.

The sad part is that if they had just kept one man from Arthur Foods, there would have been no problem. Mr. Atherne, who ran Arthur Foods for Mr. Arthur, knew every aspect of the business. He watched over the warehouses, knew where the stock went and what every stand would need the next day. He would check the stand sheets at night. He knew what the attendance would be the next day and made sure there were enough workers in the stands. With the help of Frank, the warehouse manager, everything worked.

The managers would check in our money and sheets at the office. If we had a big shortage, the sheet was run again for mistakes, and the money was re-counted. If we were still short, we would talk to Mr. Atherne.

It was simple. We didn't even mind standing in line at the office as we bantered back in forth. Sometimes, we'd be laughing so hard that it carried right into the office. During the celebration for the Statue of Liberty restoration, I wore one of the headdresses they were selling at the stadium that looked like the one on the Statue. It was large and green. I walked into the office, and a young supervisor whom I teased all the time said, "Do you see what she's wearing on her head?"

"Don't you think I look like the Statue of Liberty?" I asked.

"No," he answered. "She's been restored."

That laugh lasted a long time, and Mr. A. laughed loudest.

That where the family part came in. We had fun. When Marriott took over, it was like a cold wind blowing everything away. No family, no closeness. In the new way of doing things, we would go months and months without seeing a friend. "You're still here?" I'd say to someone when I saw them again. The fans could also feel the "corporate" atmosphere instead of the former family feel of the stadium. Groups of the regular fans would even march through the stadium chanting, "We want Arthur's, we want Arthur's." Silently, the concession workers agreed with them.

The new owners had no clue what stock to send. We'd have ten times the number of beer cups we needed. Stands would be open when they weren't needed, and no stand would be open where it was needed. Shortages were rampant, and we all had to learn to use unnecessary computers. I ran a line even though I knew they didn't want me to, just to maintain my contact with people. After looking for shortages for hours, Donna and I would get home very late.

We'd work ourselves to death, but the fans were still irate. It just didn't make sense.

The man in charge was on the hot seat. He spent a lot of time on television telling everyone the grilled hot dogs would soon return. The flagship was sailing along, but it sure looked like it was sinking to me.

We somehow made it through the first season with Marriott, one day at a time. At the end of the season we had tee-shirts made for our stand that read, "WE SURVIVED 1991!"

We all tried to remain hopeful during the off-season that the first year with Marriott was a transition year and that things would be better in 1992. The managers all attend pre-season meetings, and we were introduced to a new General Manager, a young, good-looking man who had run concessions at some other ballpark, perhaps in Chicago. I called him "The Kid," and so help me, no matter who asked him a question, he never had an answer. They ran lots of videos with concession workers in spotless uniforms with their badgers straight and spotless shoes. These videos explained what to do and what not to do, so I leaned over to Donna and asked,

"How come we get videos on what not to do when they're the ones screwing up?"

When the season began, our scheduling team of Peggy and Barbara were having nervous breakdowns. Marriott wanted their people to be involved in the scheduling, but they had no clue how to do it and would resent Peggy and Barbara. This breakdown in communication did not bode well for the season.

I decided it was a good time to try to lighten things up, so I went to one of the supervisors, the one whose mother was a concessions worker, and said, "This is depressing. What can we do to have some fun?"

"You're right, Lucy," he answered. "Maybe we can shake things up."

I thought for a while and so did Paul. I just happened to have a collection of troll dolls in the stadium and had an idea.

"What if I pretend to put a curse on your with one of the troll dolls," I suggested. "Then you come in and pretend your back is killing you."

"Yeah, that's good," he agreed excitedly.

"We'll do it right before the gates open, but we have to keep a straight face."

"Yeah, yeah, he said like a little kid.

"I went into the stand and started complaining about Paul. "I'm so mad at him," I yelled. "I just hate him. When we get set up, we're going to do a troll dance and put a curse on him."

"Okay," everyone agreed. They were used to me.

When the time came, I picked up the troll doll, and we all danced around the stand chanting like some sort of weird cult figures. We're all chanting, "Put a curse on Paul's back, put a curse on Paul's back."

When we were finished, Cookie, who has five kids, said, "Don't point that doll at me—I might get pregnant again." Of course, I pointed it right at her stomach and said, "Make Cookie pregnant!"

About an hour later, Paul came in the stand. Everyone looked around sheepishly. He reached the middle of the stand and suddenly grabbed his back.

"Ouch," he moaned. Everyone's eyes bugged out of their heads. Paul kept it up, "What a pain!"

He dragged himself to a chair in the corner and sat down. I heard Cookie yell, "Oh no, now I'm going to get pregnant again!" The crew was frozen in place, and Pat whispered, "Lucy, you got the power." Paul was still rubbing his back. Finally, he got up and moaned all the way to the door. As everyone stood watching, I suddenly yelled, "Gotcha!"

They slowly realized that they'd been had, and I heard Cookie sigh, "Thank heaven!" It was one of the best tricks I've ever played, and it came off perfect. Paul went away as happy as a little pig.

Unfortunately, it was a bright spot during a very dark period. We weren't laughing much with Marriott. The big shots had decided that sausages would be just the thing to put in our stand. *Four different kinds of sausage!* I guess they figured, the grilled Dodger Dogs are not enough trouble, so let's multiply the complexity by a factor of five. They did have a few other stands with grilled hot dogs by now, and I must admit that the sausages were delicious. A man named Jody Maroni supplied them. He was a nice young man, and every time he'd come in, we'd all sing, "Here comes Jody Maroni! Here comes Jody Maroni!" The fans seemed to like it, and so did Jody. Of course, the sausages were a giant pain. The guys in the kitchen would cook the hot dogs, then clean the grill, put on the sausages, clean the grill, then put on the sausages, and so it went.

About this time they were giving us a huge crew because they had no clue how many people we needed. There were a lot of guys in the kitchen. There was a nice man named Carlos who came to work for us. (He was a business man, and was taking time off because of stress, so he decided it would be great to work at the stadium.) He was intelligent, sweet, and very funny. It was his idea to play the radio while the guys were wrapping hot dogs. They were the good old songs, so they started singing while wrapping. They would sing to "Rollin' on the River," only they would change the words to "Rollin' 'nother hot dog." They would sing other songs, too, and I'd go back and join them. I loved those songs. So, we did have some fun, but it was a very strange time with all these workers tripping over each other. Somehow, the guys formed a very close relationship, but the whole thing was confusing and disturbing.

Carlos left at the end of the season. We hated it. He had loved working there, and it had been good for him and for us.

It was about this time that Marriott decided to get rid of the only two people who knew what they were doing—Peggy and Barbara, our scheduling team. In all honesty, by now they were ready to leave. Later, I heard that they both sued for mental stress and harassment, and they won. Now, came the string of people who tried to do scheduling, one after another, for two years. Each one was worse than the one before. Scheduling is a very important part of the concession process. Mrs. Johnson, who started with Arthur Foods, and worked for years, was the best. She knew every worker's number (Badge No.) She even remembered the day they started. Once, when she had surgery, I made a get-well card for her. Instead of having everyone sign their name, they put their number down. I knew she would know who each number was. It is so important to know these numbers, immediately. You associate the person with it. You know who it is, where they are working, and what kind of work they do. It saves so much time. When Mrs. J. left, Peggy took over and did remarkably well. Anyway, in years, they never found a person who could do scheduling. Still haven't!

The following year, they decided to bring in a crew to cook the sausages before my crew came in. It was impossible! The inventory was a mess, my shortages were a mess, and I was a mess.

The biggest goof-up Marriott pulled was the night our nice young supervisor Mike came in with a paper. He handed it to me. It was from the office, and it said that we have decided the workers in the stands will no longer stop for the National Anthem. *I* read it and tore it to pieces. Mike was actually a nice kid, and we liked each other. He gasped and left the stand. A few minutes later, I was called to the office. I picked up our union rep., just in case. The G.M. said, "Lucy, you can't tear up directives from the office."

"I can when they say that," I replied.

Mike said, "Lucy, you made me look like a fool."

"Don't bring around directives like that and you won't feel a fool," I answered. "We have always stopped and will always stop for the National Anthem in any stand I'm in."

"Can't you do it for just one night?" the G.M. asked.

The union rep. said we could do it for one night.

"Oh no, we can't!" I said. "How can you give up your principles for one night?"

I left. In ten minutes tops, another directive came around saying that we have decided we will do our patriotic duty and stop for the Anthem. I don't mean to sound like I was the cause of the second notice being sent around. In truth, almost every single manager and worker refused to accept it. Their screams were heard all over the stadium.

"The Kid" lasted two years. We (the managers) were called to a meeting in the middle of the season. A bunch of us were laughing and joking around. "The Kid" came up and said, "Lucy, I've got good news for you."

"You're leaving?" I asked.

"Yes, as a matter of fact, I am. I have an offer that's very good."

"Good luck," I said. It really did upset me that someone so unqualified for the job should make so much money. But he really was a nice kid!

The Flag Ship had sunk, and Marriott was gone. For 30 years of service, they had given me and Henny (my friend who had worked for me for years and had been there almost as long as I had) a nice clock and a glass plaque with Dodger Stadium on it.

Now, it was Aramark's turn to try. We had to go to a meeting at the Bonaventure Hotel in June of '94 in the middle of the season. "Here we go again," Donna and I said. Same kind of Big Shots running around (they were not quite so arrogant), one speech after the other, more video tapes played. Our new leader was introduced; he was left over from Marriott. I thought he probably knew a little more than the one that just left, and I could speak to him, at least. Aramark has concessions all over, and their trucks are still noticeable all over town. We were sick to death of the videos, especially the one about learning to detect someone who is drunk and not serving them. We knew it by heart. They served us dinner, and

I'll say this—it was not nearly as good as what Marriott had served.

We had a new G.M. He had worked with Marriott, and I had a pretty good rapport with him. The new concession manager was one of the supervisors who used to work for Carl's, Jr. I knew we were in trouble. Not a Clue! In all honesty, I think they did cater to me sometimes, because I was number one in seniority. I could be a real pain, sometimes. I had a feeling they said that more than once behind my back, only adding three more words after the "pain".

It seemed to us working there that Aramark didn't pay much attention. They just wanted to run the concessions from afar, check the books, and get the money. They were never around to se what was happening. I'm sure it's the same this year.

The new G.M. did fix the scheduling. He REALLY fixed it! He got someone who knew nothing about it and could not retain one single number. Not a Clue!

As I said before, scheduling is knowing the workers' badge numbers. The poor gal couldn't remember **my** number, and I was number one. Oh Lord! She didn't know where anyone belonged or where they went. I spent half my life at the scheduling table trying to find my workers. It was a nightmare. If the workers took a day off, they were moved to another stand, and just try and find out where they were. Of course, all the managers were in the same boat, and I'm sure still are. I don't fault her. She was nervous and didn't have the ability to retain anything. She probably would have done fine in another position. It's a hard job. I couldn't do it. But then again, I wouldn't try!

When the baseball players had their strike in '94—because they weren't getting enough money—it made me quite ill. How much money is enough? And where does it end? Our union asked us if we would be willing to picket for the Dodgers if they did strike. I was bitterly opposed to this. At the union meeting, I said, "I have a real problem striking for men that are making millions of dollars. The fans are the ones suffering, with the price of tickets and food going up. How can a man with a family enjoy going to see someone on the field making millions when it takes his whole paycheck to take his family to a game?"

Scott Harris printed this in his column in the L.A. Times, and quoted me. That was really nice of him. I'm certainly not the only one to feel this way, judging by the way the fans stayed away in droves. It's so sad now. They have fences so the players can't sign autographs. It is now officially a Business, not the world's greatest pastime. Of course, people come because they love the game and can't help it. I'm so happy that my family and I saw it he way it should be. But doesn't that apply to so many things today?

I do think one of the best things that happened to baseball in a long, long time was the home run race between McGwire and Sosa. It wiped away some of the bitterness of the strike, the exorbitant salaries, etc.

On Opening Night, May 8, 1995, before the game, Dodger Stadium paid tribute to the employees who had worked there the longest: security, custodians, ushers, ticket takers. Roger Owens and I represented concessions. Roger is the vendor who has been on TV a lot, with Jay Leno and Johnny Carson. He is famous for throwing bags of peanuts. It was quite a thrill to be on the field. While we were there, a news photograph^came over to take a picture of Roger for his paper.

"Can I take your picture, Roger?" he asked.

"Sure," he answered, while grabbing me around the waist and pulling me over. "Come on, Lucy. You should be in here, too."

The poor photographer had no choice. Now, I ask you, is that class, or what? The picture turned out great.

Few people know this story about Roger, but many years ago, maybe 25 or so, I worked on the Orange Level, and I would see Roger and his brother come by every day. We would always speak, and Roger had a corny joke nine times out of ten. One day, his brother came in the stand. I said, "Where's Roger?" He had a funny look on his face.

"What's wrong?" I asked.

"He's in the hospital," he answered, his head down. "In a coma. He turned over in his Jeep in training with the ROTC. They don't know if he'll come out of it."

I was shocked. I asked him to please come by every day and tell me how he's doing. It was so sad. We were all praying for him at the stadium. Each day, Roger's brother came by—no news, still in a coma. This went on for a very long time. I think it was a month later, before his excited brother came by and told me, "He woke up!"

"Oh, thank God," I said happily. "Send him my love and best wishes."

About a month later, I felt a tap on my shoulder. I turned around, and there was Roger. I put my arms around him. He could barely speak—it took him forever to mouth the words—and his walking was very unsteady. I was so glad to see him, but I wondered if he would ever be the same. Now, he throws those bags of peanuts out and is in demand everywhere. Bless his heart. All that, and he's a class act, too. But I'm afraid he still tells corny jokes.

My last two years at the stadium were the worst of my life. Attendance was down, and fans were angry about the strike—the ballplayers strike that had just been settled a while back, and people were not coming to the games. The Boss decided to close our stand. For the first time in thirty years, I went down to manage on the Yellow Level.

I was already not happy, anyway. My shortages were worse than ever, and they had moved one of my workers. I was fond of him, and he was very angry. He felt it was a reflection on him, and I don't blame him.

Another of my favorite people left. She wasn't very happy with my attitude. I wasn't happy with my attitude. Under stress all the time. I'm sure she thought I was to blame for the shortages. There wasn't enough money in the world to pay us for staying there half the night, under that stress, and to go and explain it to a person who didn't even know what he was doing. Anyway, it was the deterioration of our happy family.

Donna went with me to the Yellow Level. (Thank God, I needed someone to support me.) It's a whole different attitude down there—cold and indifferent. In the elevator, when the workers found out what stand we were going to, they moaned, "Oh no, you're not going there. They eat you up! They hate strangers coming in there." My little Peanut had already told me abut when she managed in there. They treated her horribly and made her cry.

Donna and I braced ourselves, unlocked the door, and the crew came in. We stood face-to-face with the Wicked Witches of the North. When I saw what I had to do, I almost fainted. There were six cashiers, two outside bars, one with the "Beers of the World". There was a prima donna cook, who paid no attention to me. If I asked him to do something, he would bang things against the wall. There was only one person there who acted like a human being, and that was a lovely older Black lady. It was a very busy stand. We had to make mountains of nachos before the gates opened, and the fans stand in those lines from before the game until after the fifth inning.

Now, the Wicked Witches were used to this. These Witches do not stop, they do not eat, they just go, go, go. I had to pick up money from outside bars, deliver stuff if they needed it, pick up money from the six cashiers, keep track of each one, close out the bartenders, put all the money together, count stock (Donna helped, of course), get stock if they ran out, run the sheet, etc. The first night, when we closed, I looked at Donna and said, "We'll be here until tomorrow."

When the money pick-up men came, they yelled, "Are you ready?"

"Hell, no," Donna wailed. "But do you happen to have Dr. Kevorkian's phone number?"

Boy, we needed that laugh. We were so tired when we walked to the car. Crossing the street to the parking lot, I wearily said, "Look out, Donna, a bus is coming."

She wearily answered, "Well, we can always hope it runs over us." That was two for Donna that night.

The third day, I had made up my mind. We went in the stand, and I said to Mr. Prima Donna, "Do you know what?"

He was surprised. "No, what?"

"You've got a hell of an attitude."

"What do you mean?" he growled.

"I mean, I think you should go to another stand," was my tart reply.

The Wicked Witches looked in horror and took in their breath as one person. (Maybe they were one person.) I called upstairs and the very clever scheduling lady moved him right next door.

Then I turned to the Wicked Witches and said, "You know something, ladies? You are not nice people. You treat people terribly. You should try and help newcomers to the stand. No one wants to come in here—they're afraid of you. Now, you take it for what it's worth. You really need to work on your people skills."

I knew I was in big trouble. As we worked that night, I turned to Donna and said, "I hate this place."

We did eventually go back to our stand, but by now, it was too late. The stadium I had loved so much had become a place I could not bear to be in. One day, toward the end of the season, the scheduling lady was being especially dense. She had placed one of my workers somewhere else, and I needed him badly. She couldn't understand. Throwing up my hands, I yelled, "Enough is enough." Going upstairs, mumbling all the way, I went in to see the G.M., explaining to him there was no reason not to give me my worker.

"This woman doesn't understand the job," I said. "She isn't capable of doing it. She puts people in the wrong place, and she doesn't belong in that position."

"I don't agree. She's doing a good job."

"But she doesn't even know my badge number, and I'm Number One!"

Then I heard the words, "She doesn't need to know the numbers."

Looking at him, I said, "You better watch your ass—Murdoch is coming!" and walked out.

Rupert Murdoch had just purchased the Dodgers and would take over next year. The contract with Aramark did have two more years to run, but Rupert had a history of looking into every aspect of whatever he was running. He always found a way to fix things that didn't work right.

I said to myself, "You're 71 years old, you've seen the best and you've seen the worst. It was July, and I'd stay to the end of the season. It's hard to explain the emptiness I felt, and the sadness. All the wonderful events kept coming back to me, but luckily one of the best was about to take place before I left.

It was the Fourth of July, and the stadium was packed. (Always was when they had fireworks; they put on an incredible show.) One of my usher friends yelled, "Lucy, go out before the game starts and watch the sky."

"Why?"

He answered, "The stealth bomber is going to fly over the stadium."

"Come on, Donna," I said. "It's time,"

We stood in the tunnel and looked up toward the west. We finally saw a black object, small at first. It came fast and became larger and larger until we saw the unmistakable wing shape. We did not hear a sound.

Suddenly, it was at the edge of the stadium, and then we heard the noise. It filled our entire bodies. As we looked up, it came over the stadium. It was huge and cast a giant shadow over the entire place. There was complete darkness. We looked up, and this magnificent plane was on top of us. It was incredible.

After it had passed, I looked at Donna, and she looked at me. There were tears running down our cheeks. We didn't say a word.

As I said before, all the great things that happened to me in the stadium came back. So many people I will never forget, so many touching moments, exciting games, concerts—they all played back like re-running a tape that had my life at the stadium on it.

So now it was my last day at work. I was running my line as I always did—for the last time in 36 years.